BUBBLES
POETRY FOR FUN AND MEANING

Theodore E. Wade, Jr., Editor
Elfred Lee and Norman Rockwell, Illustrations

For Norma, my good friend.
Lillian Fisher

GAZELLE PUBLICATIONS
5580 Stanley Dr., Auburn, CA 95603

ACKNOWLEDGMENT: "Mice" from FIFTY-ONE
NEW NURSERY RHYMES by Rose Fyleman.
Copyright 1931, 1932 by Doubleday & Company, Inc.
Reprinted by permission of the publisher.

Manufactured in the United States of America.
Library of Congress Catalog Card Number: 86-83029.
International Standard Book Number: 0-930192-17-6.

CONTENTS

ABOUT THIS BOOK

Fifty-four writers share their feelings and ideas through the poetry on these pages. Some of their poems are serious. A few are sad. But most are fun and happy—like bubbles!

The eighty-two poems in the main section of this book were chosen from some two thousand submitted for consideration. In the screening process, more than two hundred poems which showed promise were retained. I asked a group of children, and adults who understand children to judge them. Final selections were based largely on their evaluation. The authors have been paid for the use of their work and have not been asked to subsidize this publication in any way.

The large notes section in the back part of the book will help make the poems come to life. You will find points of interest about the authors, questions to highlight thoughts in some of the poems, notes on what inspired them, activities that use them as launching pads, and many more poems and verses.

The smaller numbers with each poem after the author's name give page numbers for quick reference to the notes. The letters *a* and *p* stand for *author* and *poem* notes.

I met Elfred Lee when we both worked in Washington, D.C. in the mid-1970s. With the tone and purpose of this volume in mind, I knew I wanted his art for it. He is now chairman of the art department at Oakwood College in Huntsville, Alabama. His wife, Sherry, manages his private studio. Their two children were models for the cover art

Dr. Donald Stoltz made the Norman Rockwell drawings available to accompany his two poems.

I almost gave this book the subtitle, "Children's poems for everyone." Obviously the poems were written for kids. I chose them for kids. I prepared the notes with kids in mind. And I requested the art for kids. But I've enjoyed the poems so much myself that I'd like to think a lot of other "big" people will, too.

Ted Wade
Editor

Poems

Bubbles Popping

Why don't bubbles ever last?
They seem to disappear so fast.
No matter where they go to play,
You can bet they'll go away.

If they fall down on the ground
They just pop without a sound.
If they float up in the sky,
You might as well tell them goodbye.

Popping, popping! everywhere,
On the ground or in the air.
Just be glad you're not a bubble,
Or you'd be in for lots of trouble!

— *Deborah Vitello*
ap 149

Balloon Moon

If the moon were a shiny

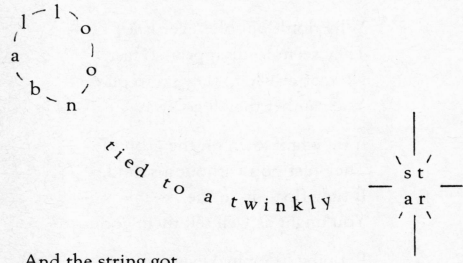

And the string got

Bro   ken,

Would it fly very far?

— Deborah Vitello
ap 149

Chasing Bubbles

I'm a speedboat, I'm a sub
Chasing bubbles round the tub.
See them bursting like balloons!
See my hands like wrinkled prunes!

— *Bonnie Kinne*
a134, p135

Mud

Slurp, slop,
Squish, squash
"Mud's all over,
You go wash!"

Splish, splash
Rinse and scrub
"Mud's off you,
Now wash the tub!"

— *Nora Norton*
a141, p142

Barefoot I Go

Barefoot I go
   in summer sun.
I skim the walk
   and then I run.
The sun has heated
   walk and street
and burns the bottoms
   of my feet.

       — *Lillian M. Fisher*
        ap122

Little Chick

Little chick
   your fluffy down
Will soon be feathers
   smooth and brown
A dainty hen
   with scarlet crown
In feathered dress
   all smooth and brown.

       — *Lillian M. Fisher*
        ap122

Poor Little Stray

Poor little stray
    where have you been?
Your coat is dull,
    your body thin.
Your tiny cat feet
    are scratched and worn.
Your tail is matted,
    one ear torn.
Dear little kitty
    you'll no longer roam.
I'll love you and feed you
    and give you a home.

— Lillian M. Fisher
a122

Sea Horse

A wee little horse
Who lives in the sea
Without any legs
Roams about free.

When he's at rest
On an ocean shelf,
He uses his tail
To anchor himself.

He looks like a horse,
But he really is not.
He can't possibly neigh
Or gallop or trot.

He's a strange little horse
At home in the sea.
Without any legs, he
Roams about free.

— *Lillian M. Fisher*
a122

Watching Clouds

It's amazing the things my mind can yield,
Lying on my back in a clover field.
When I stop and begin to stare
At the clouds up in the air,
Holding within their fleecy whiteness
Shapes my mind can bring to likeness,
Of cars, trucks and ships with sails,
And tropical fish with fanlike tails.
Daffodils and butterflies
Appear before my youthful eyes,
Dancing, waving through the skies.

It seems I've just begun to wonder
When the sky begins to thunder.
Suddenly, I must roll over
And leave my fancies with the clover,
For my mind must cease to roam;
I must hurry and run back home!

— *Julie Dansby*
a121

Special to Me

You're the one who comforts my sorrow;
In your eyes understanding I see.
You're the one who lifts my spirits;
Mom, you're special to me.

You're the one that I can have fun with;
True friends forever are we.
You're the one I can always confide in;
Mom, you're special to me.

Others may see you as "normal";
Plain to some you may be.
But when you feel common, remember
You're always special to me.

— *Julie Dansby*
AI21

I Like to Dream

I like to lie here on my back
And look up at the sky;
See the twinkling stars above,
Watch the moon pass by.

Every day I like to sit
Beneath a shady tree;
Dream of all the things I'll do
And all that I can be.

I guess I'm just a dreamer,
And Mom says it's all right
To watch a lazy river flow
Or see a bird take flight.

A little dreaming makes me happy,
Fills my heart with joy.
It's all a part of being
A happy, growing boy!

— Angie Monnens
a140, p141

I Can Travel Far

I can go 'most anywhere,
No need to take a car,
In the books I read each day,
I can travel far.

I may go around the world
Or sail across the sea,
Over hills and valleys
To lands unknown to me.

From Oregon to Zanzibar
Thru miles of desert sands.
Many lovely sights I'll see
In every strange, new land.

On its printed pages
Adventures lie ahead.
I like to read a book at night
When it's time for bed!

— *Angie Monnens*
a140

Cold Blows the Wind

Cold blows the wind
And cold it blows once more
Until the icy droplets
Form above my door

And when the wind grows tired
And goes to sleep somewhere
I look out through my window
To see the trees so bare

I bundle up real warm
So I can play outside
But then I hear it coming back
Too late for me to hide

So I pull my cap down tight
To cover up by ears
And wrap my scarf around my nose
Before the red appears

I watch the leaves dance by
And clutter up the street
And then I feel the cold come in
Around my neck and feet

Oh, cold blows the wind
And cold it blows once more
And I can't run near fast enough
To get back inside my door

— *Thomas Lynn*
ap 139

Mrs. March

I'd like to ask a question,
Mrs. March, so new,
Just how do you expect to act?
What do you plan to do?
You haven't been so very nice
on this windy day,
I wish you'd change your ways a bit,
if you plan to stay.

Why can't you be a little more
like April, meek and mild?
Why do you roar and scold so much
like a naughty child?
There's so much beautiful that you
could do, if you would try
to put a little springtime
in that winter sky.

I'd like to climb atop a hill
and whisper in your ear.
but with the wind so noisy there,
I know you'd never hear.
Now Mrs. March, let's talk this out,
then surely you'll agree
we'd like you better if you put
a green dress on each tree!

— *Marion Schoeberlein*
ap144

Conversation

The conversation
    rounds the corner of the house.

Hurried mutterings
    intermingled with stacatto comments.

The chickens
    stroll gossiping by.

               — *Auril McKenzie*
                 ap140

The Catcher Caught

Sore throat,
Cough uncontrolled,
I wasn't chasing
But I caught a cold.

Catching a germ
Is like catching a flea,
When I wasn't looking
It caught me!

               — *Edel Wignell*
                 ap153

Advice

The best advice that I can give
Comes from a centipede's mother:
Put your best foot forward
& then another & another & another
      & another & another
           & another
    & another
      & another
   & another
     & another
       & another
        & another
       & another
& another
& another
   & another
    & another & another
 & another
    & another & another
  & another
  & another

     & another

— *Louis Phillips*
ap142

A Very Fat Cat Named Patterson Pat

Patterson Pat was a very fat cat
Who lived in the Drew's corner house.
They bought him one day
From the SPCA
In hopes that he'd catch a big mouse.

Patterson Pat was a very fat cat
Who liked to go snooze in the sun.
With warmth on his fur
His motor would purr
As if to say, "Snoozing is fun."

Patterson Pat was a very fat cat
Who liked to eat supper in bed.
He'd gobble it down
And then with a frown
Try rolling the bowl with his head.

Patterson Pat was a very fat cat
Who liked to climb up tall trees.
Till the day he got stuck
And a big fire truck
Had to come to the aid of his pleas.

Patterson Pat was a very fat cat
Who liked to chase mousies for fun.
But with a tummy so round
It scraped on the ground
While his feet were still trying to run.

Patterson Pat was a very fat cat
Who sharpened his claws on the chair.
With no one in sight
He'd use all his might
Sending pieces of chair through the air.

Patterson Pat was a very fat cat
Who liked to meow in the night.
Then old Mr. Drew
Threw out a big shoe
And Patterson jumped out of sight.

Patterson Pat still lives with the Drews
Growing fatter and rounder still.
With a grin on his face
He struts 'round the place
Thinking he's king of the hill.

— *Debbie Rider Allen*
a115, p116

33

To a Small Bear

Oh Theodore, oh Theodore,
I'm sorry that your coat got torn
and that I left you on the floor,
oh Theodore.

You came to me when I was born,
you grew to be my special friend,
you were a pillow safe and warm
when Mama tucked us in, and then,

You let me cry into your fur
when I broke her best china cup.
She scolded me for that and, as
she calmly swept the pieces up,
I told her I was making tea for Theodore.

And now your fur is getting frayed
and now your tummy's squishy-soft.
I must have lost your tie one day
and hugged your brand-new buttons off,
dear Theodore.

But still you are my favorite friend
for secrets shared in your good ear
and suitcase trips to Grandma's house
and spilling out my fears.

Oh Theodore, oh Theodore,
it's sad to see you looking poor.
You just don't seem like Theodore,
my Theodore.

But I would love you quite the same
if you went by a different name.
So next time Mom says, "Time for bed,"
you mind if I just call you Ted?

— *Joan Kramer*
a135, p136

One-eyed Teddy

Sister says it's just a button,
but I know it's a teddy bear's eye.
Somewhere there's a teddy squinting
and seeing only half of the sky.

Somewhere there's a teddy sitting
squinting at far-off Mars,
enjoying the beautiful evening
but seeing only half of the stars.

I'll never find that poor teddy
with the squinting one-eyed face.
I'll never find him and put back
his eye in that vacant space.

But I'll have Mama do some sewing.
It's the best I can do, you see.
Somewhere there's a teddy with one eye
but my teddy will have three.

— *Robert D. Hoeft*
a130, p131

One Little Drum

A big-enough boy
with one little drum,
Makes a lot of tat-tat
while he's having his fun.

Up to the house
and in through the door,
Then out to the kitchen
and across the wet floor.

Over to the stove
and back to the table,
Playing tat-a-tat-tat
as fast as he is able.

Mama's on the telephone,
a finger in her ear.
How can she enjoy the drum
that she can barely hear?

Out in the living room,
it's Daddy's tough decision,
to listen to the tat-a-tat
or watch the television.

Now Mama takes the drum. . . .

— *Ted Wade*
a150, p151

A string down the middle
and a light on top,
Needs a match to start
and a puff to stop.

— *Ted Wade*
a150, p151

Blankie's Shampoo

Oh, Blankie, don't worry!
Please don't despair!
I'm right here beside you.
I know it's not fair
For you to be put
In the washing machine
Just 'cause *they* think
You should be clean.
Oh, Blankie, remember
I didn't want you
To have to get this
Awful shampoo!
You heard me try
So hard to tell
Them not to wash you;
That I like your smell!
But they wouldn't listen
To what I said;
They said you had
To be washed before bed.

But I promise you, Blankie,
I'll try harder to
Prevent you from getting
Another shampoo!

— *Babs B. Hajdusiewicz*
a128, p129

Bill and Jim and Joe and Zack

Bill and Jim and Joe and Zack
All wanted to sit way back in the back.
The driver said no, that could not be,
There were no seat belts there, you see.
The driver said they would have to sit
In seats where seat belts would all fit.
So Bill and Jim and Joe and Zack
Rode safely in seat belts, *not* in the back.

— *Babs B. Hajdusiewicz*
a128

My Turn to Talk

My hand goes up when I want to say
Something that happened to me today.
I wait so patiently until
It's time for the others to be still.
I wait and wait to have my say
About what happened to me today.
Then suddenly I look around
And you know what? There isn't a sound!
All my friends are looking at me
And waiting, ever so patiently.
They're waiting to hear what I have to say
About what happened to me today.
But, guess what! Oh, no! It couldn't be!
I've forgotten my story of what happened to me!

— *Babs B. Hajdusiewicz*
a128, p129

My Organs

My heart pumps my blood
From my head to my toes.
All over my body
My blood goes and goes.

My brain lets me think;
It explains what I see.
It stores all the facts
My teacher gives me.

My lungs breathe the air
That keeps me alive.
I've learned all of this
And I'm only five!

And now that I know
What these organs are for,
I'll be wearing my seat belt
And locking my door.

Then just in case
My car is crashed;
My organs stay safe,
Not ripped up or smashed!

— *Babs B. Hajdusiewicz*
a128, p129

I'm Three

I used to wear diapers
I slept in a crib
I sat in a high chair
And I wore a bib.

But now I'm lots bigger
I have a big bed
I don't wear diapers
I have a potty instead.

I sit at the table
Like big people do
I don't need a bib
When I eat my stew.

I'm not a wee baby
As I once used to be
I'm a big person now
I'm three, three, three!

— *Babs B. Hajdusiewicz*
a128

I'm Four

When I was three
I couldn't do
So many things
I wanted to.

I couldn't go down
The street to play
With my friend, Seth
He lives a long way!

He lives four houses
Down from me.
He's my best friend
And so, you see,

I'd rather play
With Seth than eat,
Except when Mom
Serves my favorite treat.

It's then I say
Goodbye to Seth
And run home fast
All out of breath.

I gobble down
My food so quick;
My mom's afraid
I might get sick.

She asks me to
Slow down a bit;
But Seth is waiting,
I just can't sit!

That hole that we
Just started to dig
Needs my shovel and me
If it's to get big!

So I chug down my milk
And bolt out the door;
My best friend's waiting!
Am I glad I'm four!

— *Babs B. Hajdusiewicz*
a128

The Rudes

The Rudes don't know or even care
When they are getting into your hair.
They interrupt when you are talking;
Their behavior is absolutely shocking!
They pinch, they hit;
They scratch, they spit.
They don't play fair when they are "it."

The Rudes, they are so terribly rude!
They open their mouths when their food's half-chewed.
They pick their noses in public places;
They stick out their tongues and make ugly faces.
They bite, they fight;
They seem to delight
In showing *you* how to not be polite.

Rudes love to eat soup, but how they slurp!
There's never "excuse me" when Rudes burp!
They don't remember a "thank you" to say
When you give them a gift on their special day.

They stare, they swear;
They seldom share.
They make fun of you and pull your hair.

They'll call you names like stupid and dumb.
You know, Rudes are really quite troublesome!
And that's not all, listen carefully now:
Rudes try real hard to get *you* somehow
To join their club
And be a Rude;
If you say "no," you'll be pursued.

They'll try their best to get your attention.
To them, rude behavior is a nifty invention!
They'll teach you all the tricks of the trade
So *you* can march in their Rude parade.
They're crude, they're shrewd;
They want *you* as a Rude.
Will you join their club? Will *you* be a Rude?

— *Babs B. Hajdusiewicz*
a128, p129

Bug Watching

There's no bigger attraction
At three years or four
Than watching a bug
On the porch floor.

Something about him
Makes you wonder then
Where he is going
and where he has been.

You know you can't touch him.
Mom's told you hands off.
But couldn't you just
Pick him up with a cloth?

If you follow him, maybe
He'll go down that crack.
But if he goes in,
Will he ever come back?

Can you remember
At three years or four,
Just watching a bug
Crossing the floor?

— *La Donna Lane Grigsby*
a 126, p 127

Pet Names

I had a dog named Broomcorn.
His fur was just like straw.
His tail would wildly wave about
No matter who he saw.

I had a cat named Mittenfizz
Who slept in the sun all day.
Then when the darkness settled in,
She would go out to play.

I even had a blue-green bird,
A parakeet, I think,
Who took a bath in a candy dish.
I named him Tiddleywink.

My turtle's name was Gumbermole,
My fish was Samson-Red.
What kind of names would you expect
From a kid called Freckle-head.

— *Marianne Filby*
a121, p122

I Likes Me

I look in the mirror
and what do I see?
Me, looking back at Me.

I talk to myself
and what do I hear?
The sound of my voice
coming into my ear.

If I'm trying to please
or not to sneeze,
I feel it in my bones.

When I take a hike
or ride a bike,
the rest of me groans.

When I think a thought,
whether good or not,
my brain stores it on a shelf.

It's a good thing for Me
that I likes Me
as I can't keep a thing from myself.

— *Rita Smith*
a146

Today, Maybe

Today's the day
   I'm running away.
I've told my mom I'm going.
She said that's fine
   just drop a line
to keep her in the knowing.
I'm packed and ready.
    I've got my teddy.
I didn't bring a light.
But that's okay
   'cause it's still day,
And I'll be back by night.

— *Rita Smith*
a146

Boring Baby

A new baby has come into the house.
I'm told I must keep quiet as a mouse,
I mustn't run or slam the door.
I hardly watch TV anymore.

When I go to school, she's being fed.
When I come back home, she's in her bed.
There are bottles and diapers everywhere
And more bibs and jammies than she can wear.

All day long she makes hardly a sound.
She's not much fun to be around.
I'm told she's quite too young to talk,
But during the night, she sure can squawk.

— *Rita Smith*
ap 146

Scared Silly

I was scared
The other day.
Parents went out
To spend Dad's pay.

House was empty
Except for me.
Then the noise,
So I went to see.

Scared silly,
I called the cops.
How embarrassing . . .
noisy raindrops!

— *Richard L. Sartore*
a144

Cat Tricks

Have you ever tried to teach a cat to sit?
Or to beg?
Or to play dead?
Or to shake its paw?
Or to roll over?

If so, you already know what happened!

— Richard L. Sartore
a144

The Color of Skin

The color of skin is hard to describe
It's just not the same for all things alive.
There's a color for you, and a color for me
And a color for tuna fish deep in the sea.

Now, let me think. . .
White people are white
No, that can't be right!
For white people aren't *white*
Like a bed sheet so bright.
And black people aren't *black*
Like coal in a sack.
And yellow people aren't *yellow*
Like a banana that's mellow.
And red people aren't *red*
Like ketchup on bread.

Wait! I've got it!

The color if skin is *not* hard to describe
It's just that it's *different* for all things alive.
God made a color for you, and a color for me
And a color for tuna fish deep in the sea.

That's the answer
And I think that it's *true!*
Tell me, now . . .
Don't you think so, too?

— *Geoffrey Stamm*
ap148

Babysitting

Back and forth
   And forth and back
I wheel the baby's stroller.

And when she cries
   I've got to stop
And sing songs to console her.

Now you see me
   Now you don't
We're playing peek-a-boo.

The game is pretty silly
   But there's nothing else to do.

I'm getting bored
   With baby-sister-sitting every day.
I'd like to put a stamp on her
   and send her far away.

Hey wait!
   My sister just looked up
      And gave me her first smile.

I guess she's not so big a pain—
   I'll keep her for a while.

        — *Constance Andrea Keremes*
           ap132

Raindrop Regiment

There's an army on the roof tonight,
　I can hear the marching feet.
They've been marching now for hours,
　Showing no sign of retreat.

It's the regiment of raindrops
　Pitter patter, here they come!
Tapping out a rousing march song
　To a thunder-thumping drum.

'Cross the roof and down the window,
　Oh, this army shows no fear.
They'll march bravely all the night long,
　'Til the dawn makes gray skies clear.

Then that regiment of raindrops
　Sadly will no longer be,
But they'll leave behind a rainbow
　As their flag of victory.

— Constance Andrea Keremes
ap132

Water's Fun—Or Is It?

Boys like to splash in puddles.
They like to wade in brooks.
They'd rather go out swimming
Than stay home reading books.

Some boys play with hoses
And run through sprinkler spray,
Or squirt their water pistols
At people in their way.

They seem to look for water
Down each and every path.
Then why do they protest so much
When asked to take a bath?

— *Helen Bradford*
a118, p119

Because I Am a Child

If I were a bird
   I'd play all day
   in the bright blue sky
I'd swing in the trees
   and hide in the leaves
   and build a nest
But most of all I'd fly
   because
That's what birds do best
If I were a bird.

If I were a fish
   I'd play all day
   in my big sea gym
I'd dive between rocks
   and hide in sea weed
   and splash the waves' crest
But most of all I'd swim
   because
That's what fish do best
If I were a fish.

If I were a frog
   I'd play all day
   in the cattail clumps
I'd croak and blink
   and hide in the mud
   and eat insect pests
But most of all I'd jump
   because
That's what frogs do best
If I were a frog.

Because I am a child
   I play all day
   wherever I may be
I jump in the clumps
   I fly in the sky
   I swim in the sea
Because I can imagine me
   being
What I want to be
Because I am a child.

— *Sharon Kuebler*
ap 137

Lion

I think that's a lion
I see over there.
I can tell by its tail
and its mane and its claws

and its yellow-brown fur
and the way that it hides
in the grass and I know
it's a lion.

It's looking at me.
Yes, those *are* lion eyes
and sharp lion teeth
and a lion-type roar,

and I'm *sure* it's a lion,
it's running like one.
And I'm sure I am leaving,
right now!

— *Robert King*
a 132, p133

Giraffe

Brown and yellow
  Yellow and brown
Quiet and tall
  up and down—
We call this animal
  Giraffe.
We call the baby one
  A calf.

The calf can see
  From far to wide
But hurries to
  Its mother's side
(And underneath
  If danger's near!)
And stays until
  The way is clear.

— *Robert King*
a 132, p 134

I'm a Kitty Cat

I like to pretend sometimes
That I'm a kitty cat.
I crawl around the floor and meow,
Then jump in Grandma's lap.

Then Grandma strokes me on my back
And gives my head a pat,
But if I want to play too long
She says, "Enough! Now scat!"

— *Martha H. Daniel*
a120

Little Ant
Why must you build
    That sandy
Teeny, weensy hill?
    But don't stop now,
You're almost through.
    I guess that hill
Is home to you. . .

— *Johnny Ray Moore*

Old Steam Train

The train is chugging down the track
   CHUG-A-CHUG-CHUUUUUG
Hugging the rails as it lugs the mail.

The train is puffing through a tunnel
   PUFF-A-PUFF-PUFFFFF
Roaring a song as it glides along.

Its whistle gives a toot
   TOOTLE-TOOT-TOOOOOT!
Nearing a road as it bears its load.

It winds around a bend
   CHUFF-A CHUFF-CHUFFFFF
Slowing down as it enters town.

Into a station it crawls
   SCREECH-A-SCREECH-SCREEEEECH
Grinding its brakes as a rest it takes.

The locomotive gives a jerk
   CLICKETY-CLACK-CLAAAACK
Then flashing a light, it rolls out of sight.

— *Howard Goldsmith*
ap125

Ginger Ale

When I was young we had a pup,
      whose name was Ginger Ale,
With floppy ears and big brown eyes
      and a little stubby tail.
The smartest little pooch around,
      she knew all her dont's and do's
But the only thing she never learned,
      was to fetch the morning news.

"Ginger, Ginger, get the paper!"
      Was a plea I made for years,
But the only thing that Ginger did
      was flap her floppy ears.

When I got a little older
      and I learned to read and write,
I showed Ginger all I knew,
      she was so very bright.
I taught her how to speak and count
      and sit and jump and beg.
But when the newsboy came along,
      Ginger Ale played dead.

"Ginger, Ginger, get the paper!"
        was our common family cry
But the only thing that Ginger did,
        was blink a big brown eye.

When I got to high school
        and made the football team,
Ginger was our mascot
        and barked with every scream.
And when we won the championship
        and my name was in bold print,
Ginger picked the paper up,
        then did a sudden sprint.

"Ginger, Ginger, drop that paper!"
        I followed her to no avail.
My headlines vanished near some bushes,
        torn to shreds by Ginger Ale.

By now my mind was really made up,
        determination streaked my face.
Ginger must retrieve the paper
        and bring it to the proper place.
So I got an old newspaper,
        tied with a piece of string,
Then I put a rope on Ginger
        and started coaxing—"Fetch and bring!"

"Ginger, Ginger, there's the paper,
      bring it and you'll get a treat."
"Come on girl, there's nothing to it,
      stand right up and move those feet."

And finally, after many hours,
      many days and many weeks,
Ginger suddenly got the message
      and started listening to my speech.
But my joy came abruptly to an end,
      just when victory was mine.
Ginger proudly brought our paper,
      plus another eight or nine.

"Ginger, Ginger, forget the paper,
      the neighbors all have given warning."
Now I must get up at seven
      to return their papers every morning.

— *Dr. Donald R. Stoltz*
ap 148

Apple a Day

An apple a day keeps the doctor away,
And apples make wonderful pie.
When a kid places one on a teacher's desk,
He's the "apple" of her eye.

An apple crushed can be eaten as sauce.
An apple squeezed becomes juice.
An apple baked is a baked apple of course,
And an apple pureed is a mousse.

Apples are peeled and seeded and sliced,
And made into dumplings and strudel.
They're cut up with salad or raisins and nuts
And served with meat, fish or noodles.

Yes, the versatile apple is man's favorite fruit,
and it can keep the doctor away.
But when covered with caramel and placed on a stick
The dentist stays busy all day.

— Dr. Donald R. Stoltz
a148

Cool Is Not So Hot

After school, in the schoolyard, just the other day,
A big kid came up to me and whispered, "Hey!
You wanna buy somethin' that'll make you real cool?
Forget all the hassle that you get in school?
Your friends are all doin' it—spaced is the word,
What's 'a matter, Kid, are you some kinda nerd?
I'll tell you what; real generous, that's me,
I'll let you try one of these babies for free!"
And he pressed into my hand a funny looking pill
Saying, "Take it, Pal, it'll give you a thrill.
When you're ready for more to zap your blues,
I'll give you a price that you can't refuse."
As he drove off in a flashy car with stripes and chrome,
I trashed that stupid pill and headed for home.
Next morning, in the paper, was a picture of this guy,
His car had wrapped a pole while he was driving "high,"
And I guess he was right, dead right, the fool,
'Cause now there's no doubt; he is cool—*real cool!*

— *Ann Gasser*
a123

Nature's Magician

Last summer, in our garden,
On a lacy dill weed,
A big green caterpillar
Crawled up to feed.

He soon stopped eating
And began to spin
A neat brown coat
He could wrap himself in.

For a few weeks he looked
Like a leaf, all dried,
And I was sure
That he had died.

But today he crawled out
And flew off to the sky—
He is now a swallowtail
Butterfly!

— *Ann Gasser*
a123

Cottontail Secret

In the corner of our yard
I was playing gardener
When I found a scooped-out place
Filled with brown rabbit fur.

I said to myself,
"Here's a rabbit nest, I think,"
'Cause I saw three tiny bunnies
All wiggly and pink.

Their nest was hidden,
But not very much,
And I knew I could look
But I mustn't touch.

Early each evening
As day lost its light,
Mother Rabbit would come
And stay all night.

This morning in the garden
I see something—what is it?
Those cute baby rabbits
Are returning my visit.

But I won't say a word,
Not even a teeny,
'Cause those rabbits are eating
My dad's prize zucchini!

— Ann Gasser
a123

Stinker and the Bandits

One Halloween like none before,
Three raccoons were at our door.
Their eyes were bright, their faces masked;
While two stayed back, the big one asked.

We gave them bread and bits of bun.
That Halloween was super fun!
"Good-bye," we said and closed the door,
But hands reached up to beg for more.

Then black as night, with stripes of white,
Their plume-tailed friend came into sight.

"Trick or treat. Trick or treat!
Give us something good to eat!"

— *Lois Kromhoff*
ap136

Tonight

Quarter moon
Shines tonight,
Stars in sky
Oh so bright,
Cricket's song,
Cool fresh air,
Oh so still,
Everywhere.

— *Merle Ray Beckwith*
ap117

Erica . . . ME

I remember who I was when I was three,
And now that I'm five, I'm simply *me*.
But who will I be when I'm thirty or sixty,
Like my mother or aunt or my grandmother Lee?
I can't imagine that woman I'll be,
The grownup my friends will someday see . . .
I'm sure that *she* certainly won't be *me*.

— *Robert D. San Souci*
ap143

Arabella

Once I had a doll I loved,
   Arabella was her name.
   Her eyes were beads, her hair was yarn
   I loved her just the same.
I carried her to bed with me,
   I took her out to play,
   But once I left her in the yard
   Until the next day!

I had a little dog as well
   Who loved my dolly, too.
   But every time he kissed her
   All he did was chew.
He showed his love that evening
   While I was tucked in bed,
   For when I woke to get my doll,
   Alas! She had no head!

— *Martha E. Whittemore*
a152, p153

Etched in Black

Last night in quiet dignity
    against the sunset glow,
Six lonely hen pheasants
    crossed my garden in the snow;
The covering drifts had led them
    with a courage hunger born
to leave their sheltered meadows
    for the upland fields of corn.
I do not chide the huntsmen who
    shot their gorgeous mates,
Nor blight with disapproval any
    festive dinner plates;
I only say that, etched in black
    against the sunset glow,
Six lonely hen pheasants crossed
    my garden in the snow.

— *Helen C. Smith*
ap 145

Silly Sleep Sheep

One sheep, two, sheep, three sheep, four. . .
There must have been a million more!
As I lay there wanting sleep,
I counted all those silly sheep.
They didn't jump the fence for me
but gathered all around to see
if I would jump the fence instead
so all of them could go to bed!

— *Helen C. Smith*
ap145

Contented Fish

Three little fish swam 'round in a tank.
First they swam up and then they sank.
They went to the bottom to stir up the sand.
(They lived only in water and never on land.)
Down to the very bottom they went
And that is the way their lives were spent.
Up and down and round and round
Without ever making one whiff of a sound.
They liked their water so cool and dank,
These three little fish that lived in a tank.

— *Auril Wood*
a154

Bus Ride

Clunketty bump,
the bus rolls;
clunketty clunketty
over the ruts and the tracks and the holes
clunketty bump it goes.

— *Nita Penfold*
ap 142

No Purpose Porpoise

I'm Percy the Playful Porpoise,
I frolic on the sea,
Though I travel in a school,
Nobody teaches me!

I'm Percy the Playful Porpoise,
I splash and play with glee,
A porpoise without purpose,
What shall become of me?

— *Joan Bellinger*
a 118

No One Came to Claim Him

A little dog, one morning,
Came to my back door,
And though he was quite dirty,
No one could love him more.

I took him in and fed him
And washed away the dust.
I tried to find who owned him
For surely someone must.

He seemed to be so grateful
For the bath and for the food,
As if he tried to tell me
That he was mine for good.

No one had come to claim him
As he was left to roam.
I'm glad he came to my back door
For now he has a home.

— *Terry Zabor*
a154

No More Kitten

Once I had a kitten
So fuzzy and so round
He fit into my pocket
And hardly made a sound.

His eyes were colored yellow
And his fur was shiny black.
If anything moved by him,
He would suddenly attack.

This playful little kitten
Would curl up on my lap
Whenever he got tired,
Just to take a little nap.

I'd hold him closer to me
And listen to him purr
And sing to him a lullaby,
Then stroke his long black fur.

I called this kitten Piggy,
'Cause he really loved to eat
Breakfast, lunch and dinner
and, in between, a treat.

I used to like to dress him
And take him for a walk.
I don't know if he liked it.
Because he couldn't talk.

I no longer have this kitten;
I must sadly tell you that.
But I'm happy to announce instead
My great big Piggy Cat.

— *Terry Zabor*
ap 154

Playing in Puddles

Thunder bang!
Lightning flash!
After the rain
I love to splash
   In the puddles.

With bare feet
I run to the street
Then like a bird
Jump from the curb
   Into puddles.

Why get alarmed
For what's the harm
If I get
A little wet
   Playing in puddles?

— Debbie Rose
ap143

Walking in the Rain

I thought I'd see umbrellas
And people slushing by,
But everyone is safe indoors
Intent on keeping dry.

Now I can walk in puddles,
I wore my boots today,
The rain and I are free to go
Where mud and bullfrogs play.

People watch from windows
But why should I explain?
I could be safe and dry myself
But I *like* to walk in rain.

— *Vera Koppler*
a135

Body Parts

My arms are up   (raise arms high)
My head is down   (bow head)
My legs walk
    all around.   (walk in a circle)

My ears are here   (hands on ears)
My eyes are closed   (hands cover eyes)
My fingers are
    upon my nose.   (fingers touch nose)

My feet I stamp   (stamp feet)
My hands I clap   (clap hands)
My knees I give
    a little slap.   (slap knees)

My back I reach   (pat back over the shoulders)
My stomach I pat   (pat stomach with hand)
And that's all
    there is to that.   (swing both arms upward)

— *Delores Davis*
ap121

Annie, Be My Friend

Annie, do come out and play;
Will you be my friend today?
Ask you mother if you can,
For I have a great big pan.
Mommy says that we can play
With it in my yard today.
Water, cups and jar tops
Are waiting in my sandbox.

Now we're sitting in the sand
Mixing, patting with our hands.
It's so much fun for us to make
Goodies for the sun to bake.

How many cookies do I have in all?
Come and see, Annie, but do not fall.
Oh Annie! look where you sat.
Now my cookies are really flat.
Oh Annie! as you got up
You stepped right on my best red cup.
Oh Annie! you walked on my cake,
Nothing's left for the sun to bake.

Mommy says it's getting late
You must go home, your mother waits;

And don't forget to wash your hands
For we've been playing in the sand.
Even though our food's not done
We did have a lot of fun.
Annie, do come back and play
And be my friend another day.

— *Delores Davis*
a121

Hop-Toad

As I was walking
   down the road,
I was followed by
   a little hop-toad.

I walked and ran;
   he jumped and hopped,
And now and then
   the two of us stopped.

He couldn't walk
   and run like me,
So I hopped and jumped
   the same as he.

— *Dorothy Golub*
ap126

Bedtime

Sometimes I think,
    when going to bed,
That I'd rather be out
    playing baseball instead,

Or digging for worms,
    or climbing a fence,
Because going to bed
    just doesn't make sense.

I'd like to be out
    having fun with a kite.
And sailing a boat
    would suit me just right.

Then along comes the morning
    and strange as it seems,
I find that I've done
    all those things in my dreams.

— *Dorothy Golub*
ap 126

What's Inside?

I wish I knew
   what is inside
The Christmas box
   all ribbon-tied.

I wouldn't mind
   you see, one bit,
Except my name's
   all over it!

       — Glenda Stroup Smithers
       ap 147

Leaf Bed

Do you like to shuffle
   through the leaves
When they're brown
   and ankle deep?

Do you like to pretend
   they're a bed
Of crinkly red
   on which to sleep?

       — Glenda Stroup Smithers
       ap 147

Smile

Smile while you're here and be happy,
and make someone else happy too.
A smile or kind word always takes
so little time for you.

Smile and give a helping hand
to someone along the way.
Be a friend; help lift the load
each and every day.

Smile and say, "I'll do my best."
That's all anyone can do.
A worthwhile effort once it's made
is reward enough for you.

Smile and keep on smiling.
Don't let that frown show through.
A smile will make so many friends,
and keep you happy too.

— *Mimas Seidenstucker Conrad*
ap119

Quiet Friend

Mighty old oak
How gracious you stand
Arms outstretched over the land.
Tossing your leaf-covered limbs
In the wind
You are truly a child's quiet friend.

— *Martha Clark Lentz*
ap 138

Birding Hints

Start your bird walk at a slow pace.
Wear faded clothes, it's no disgrace.
Be patient, walk quietly, and don't leave a trace.
Keep the sun to your back and your arms in place.
As you wait, be aware, see insects take chase.
See spider webs woven like intricate lace.
If you do these things like a birding ace,
You and a bird may come face to face.

— *Maurine Armour*
a116, p117

Fourteen Cats

Mrs. Stairs owned fourteen chairs
And fourteen cats as well,
The chairs were soft as teddy bears
And comfy—you could tell.

Mrs. Stairs, caught unawares
Came home one sunny day
To find the cats in all the chairs
Which filled her with dismay.

Mrs. Stairs gave hostile glares
"I don't like this a bit.
With fourteen cats on fourteen chairs
There's no place I can sit."

Mrs. Stairs was one who shares
But not This Much, she thought,
"Get off!" she snapped, and down they jumped
Annoyed that they'd been caught.

— *Eileen Ellen Murphy*
ap141

The Cat With the Cauliflower Ear

There once was a cat, a pretty little cat,
All gold and white and fluffy.
She always looked immaculate
And never, never scruffy.
Her family called her "Precious,"
Which strangers thought most queer,
Because this dainty little cat
Had a cauliflower ear.
Now everyone knows that deformities
And other handicaps
Can lead the unobservant
And unthinking into traps.
They never scratch the surface
To find what lies below
And thus may reach conclusions,
How wrong they never know.

So it was with Precious,
This gentle little cat.
They labelled her a fighter,
Never knowing that
Surgery, not fighting,
Caused her deformity.
So never base your judgment
Just on what you see.

— *Betsy Craig*
a119, p120

Heads bobbing like corks,
Ten baby ducklings follow
Mama on the pond.

— *Betsy Craig*
a119, p120

Clouds

White, fluffy clouds
          Dance in the air,
They're lovely things,
          Beyond compare,
Tumbling in the
          Sky so wide,
They're much too big
          To ever hide.
But, when they're dark
          We won't complain.
They bring the earth
          A drink of rain.

— Janet Geiger
a 123, p124

Woodpecker Hill

There's a wonderful racket on Woodpecker Hill!
From earliest morning till night
each red-headed resident uses his bill
to tatoo every object in sight!
The first to get started arrive in a bunch
and probe for their breakfast with care.
The second platoon moves in shopping for lunch—
which becomes an ear-splitting affair!
The afternoon crew, clearly out for a lark,
soundly rat-a-tat-tats every tree
scaring dozens of bugs hidden deep under bark
where they thought they were safe as could be!
But the group that dines late lingers on for the fun
of exploring. They hammer and thump
every crevice and cranny; then before they are done,
make a drum of a hollowed-out stump!

There's no moment, in fact, that finds everything still
until night falls at last upon Woodpecker Hill.

— *Emina Wesner*
ap 152

Bicycle Parade

Jennifer Joan felt like jumping and dancing
All over the place when Father said, glancing
From news he was reading to Mother, "My dear,
The Fourth of July will be splendid this year!
The town has a number of plans under way
For events so exciting that this holiday
Will be one to remember!" "Indeed!" Mother said,
While jubilant Jennifer stood on her head!

"Downtown, bright and early, we'll sit in the stands
For music and marching by brass-buttoned bands!"
"I'll march," Jenny offered, "and carry the flag!"
"Much too short," declared Father. "You might let it drag!"

"At the fairgrounds a man with a mammoth balloon
Has agreed to fly passengers all afternoon!"
"May I take a ride?" begged J.J. with a skip.
"Sorry, dear," Mother frowned. "It's too dangerous a trip!"

"A picnic will follow with ice cream and cake,
Topped off by a fireworks display from the lake!"
But whenever Jennifer put in a word,
"Too young" or "too little" was all that she heard!

No one was much sadder than Jennifer Joan
As she slipped out-of-doors to go thinking alone,
How she and her friends could help celebrate, too.
They came one by one—the whole neighborhood crew.
They got off their bicycles, tricycles, and
All sat on the steps to give Jenny a hand.
They clapped when she told them, "It's easy as pie!
I know what we'll do on the Fourth of July!"

That day they cut paper strips—red, white and blue—
Trimmed their wagons and tricycles—bicycles, too.
The show started off with J. J. in the lead
As they rode up the hill at a dignified speed.
When they got to the top, she circled in back,
And proudly the next one in line led the pack!

Long streamers of red, white and blue took the breeze
To flutter from handlebars and wrap around knees.
While bright colors whirled with each turn of the wheels,
The kids rode to music of giggles and squeals!
Beaming mamas and papas, who watched from the shade
All cheered when they saw the Bicycle Parade!

— Emina Wesner
ap 152

108

Wishful Thinking

Some days I just wish to sail out on the seas,
When my friends seem to vanish in twos and by threes;
Because I'm not pretty, with blonde, curly hair,
They seem not to notice the niceness that's there.

If only they'd stop just to talk for a while,
Perhaps then they'd notice my spectacular smile!
I'd share all my secrets and stop playing pretend
If only I had my own special friend.

— *Pearl Bloch Segall*
a144, p145

Another book report is due,
and there's a test in math next week.
I need a miracle from you, Dear Lord,
if you don't mind.

Say what?
I should study for the test?
Read the book? Do my best?
Then you'll help me remember what I've learned?
Well . . .
That sounds fair,
long as I know that you'll be there.

— *Nikki Grimes*
ap 127

TV Waits

I love to watch TV at night
Before I go to bed,
But Mom tells me to take a bath
And then shampoo my head.

Then all my homework must be done
Before it gets too late,
And when I'm through my eyes droop shut,
TV will have to wait!

— *Wallis C. Adams*
ap 115

Bubbles

Bubbles bubbles everywhere,
Floating gently in the air,
Big and fat or very small,
With bright colors in them all.
Blowing bubbles is such fun,
I hope that we are never done.

— *Wallis C. Adams*
ap 115

Notes

Wallis C. Adams

Wallis Adams enjoys poetry because her father, Rex Mobley, did. He was a professional wrestler and also a well-published poet—an interesting combination. He wrote more than a thousand poems.

Poetry is not all that Mrs. Adams enjoys. She is the mother of ten children, five of which were adopted. Some have grown up and now have children of their own.

TV Waits

Have you ever wanted to do one thing but had to do something else? This happens all through life, and most people soon learn to be happy with the choices they make. What probably made the child who couldn't watch TV happy?

Bubbles

We chose a bubbles poem to begin this book, and with this poem we finish it. You might like to compare the two. And if you look through the pages, you will find a third poem about bubbles. "Bubbles" seemed like a nice word to choose for the title.

Debbie Rider Allen

In her work, Debbie Allen writes and designs printed material for a public relations firm in Richmond, Virginia. She also helps get information about her clients out to the public through television, radio and newspapers.

When she is not in her office, she likes to play her cello in a local orchestra, to swim and water ski and to keep the inside of her house bright and green with many kinds of plants.

A Very Fat Cat Named Patterson Pat

If you enjoy rhythm and word pictures, you probably had fun reading about Patterson Pat. Notice how each of the eight stanzas are alike. And within each stanza, you can also see repeated rhythm. The pattern of strong and weak sounds is almost like that of a limerick. Here is a sample limerick from an unknown author.

> There was an old man of Peru
> Who dreamed he was eating his shoe.
>   He woke in the night
>   In a terrible fright,
> And found it was perfectly true.

Lines one, two and five are alike. How many strong sounds does each one have? How many strong sounds are in line three and in line four? Now look at the cat poem and count the strong sounds in each line. Strong-sound patterns are explained more in the note about the poem "Chasing Bubbles."

"Patterson Pat was a very fat cat." What makes this line fun to read? What sound is most repeated? How many times?

Would you like to make up another stanza for the poem?

Patterson never was a real cat except in imagination, but a neighbor who once lived next door to the author got her to thinking about cats. Every morning he would take his five cats out in his front yard, two at a time, on leashes. It must have been funny to watch.

By the way, SPCA stands for Society for the Prevention of Cruelty to Animals.

Maurine Armour

"I was raised on a small ranch in California's San Joaquin Valley and have loved birds and nature since childhood.

"I enjoy teaching children about the kinds of birds they might see in their yards, and I sometimes use poetry to help them remember. Birding is an inexpensive hobby that can last a lifetime. A child who becomes aware of birds often also develops an interest in the whole out-of-doors.''

Birding Hints

I have included Maurine Armour's poem in the collection because it is an invitation to a kind of outdoor pleasure you may not have thought of. To many poeple, a bird is a bird. If you want to step into a new world, go for an early morning walk with someone who knows birds.

Maurine Armour explains an interesting bit of background to the poem's last line, "You and a bird may come face to face."

"A nine-year-old boy in one of my beginning birding classes had just such an experience. I had told him that if he would sit quietly by a certain shrub, he might come face to face with a bird. A white-crowned sparrow did come out, sit on a twig and look him in the face. Jim is now [May 1985] twenty-one and an avid birder. I long ago became the student and he the teacher.''

Merle Ray Beckwith

After graduation from Western Michigan State University, Merle Beckwith went to Nigeria as a Peace Corps Volunteer. Then after graduate study in anthropology and education, he taught for a few years. Beginning in 1971, he traveled around the United States for six years working his way.

Now he and his wife live in Santa Barbara, California. He writes poetry and song lyrics as well as working for the Association for Retarded Citizens.

Tonight

Read this poem slowly trying to take in the feeling of the peaceful evening. Mr. Beckwith could have used more words. For example, he might have written: "A quarter moon is shining tonight. The stars are so bright up in the sky. . . ." Why do you think fewer words made the poem better?

As an activity, imagine a scene (or better yet, go and view one) such as a sail boat crossing a lake, and imitate Beckwith's style. Make each word carry a full load of meaning. When you come to the end, go back and find unnecessary words to chop out, keeping a smooth flow of sound.

Beckwith originally called the poem, "Evening." He explains how it came about: "One night when the moon was one-quarter full, my wife asked me to take out the trash. As I walked, the moon, stars, air and crickets filled my heart with this poem. When I got back inside the house, I recited 'Evening' to my wife. I feel it illustrates a feeling of harmony with the universe."

Joan Bellinger

Joan is a free lance writer working at home in Burnaby, British Columbia. She specializes in travel, history and poetry, as well as in children's stories and poems. She enjoys most, sitting outside in her beautiful garden writing for children. Weeds in the garden provide necessary exercise. She pretends pulling them up is editing.

Every day Joan Bellinger writes something, if only a grocery list, and she is an avid postman watcher. She has published articles in England, Canada and the United States.

Helen Bradford

After Helen Bradford's own two children grew up and left the home nest, she spent her time providing day care for a number of others. Now she and her husband are retired, but she still does volunteer work at an elementary school in Salt Lake City. To help her second graders celebrate holidays, she makes cookies. Her small yard is "worked to the limit," and when it's cold outside she knits ski sweaters and baby sets. Then between and among and around all that she writes poems—and types them out by the one-finger method. She began writing poems when she was eight years old.

Water's Fun—Or Is It?

It's true that most boys like to play with water and do other active things. And girls usually do enjoy reading. But many boys like books, too, and nothing is wrong with girls that like to run or play in water sprinklers. Kids that can enjoy many different activities have the most fun.

Mimas Seidenstucker Conrad

Mimas came to the United States from Germany. She and her four daughters now live in Southern California. "Accounting has been my profession," she explains, "but writing for children my desire." She is also a pilot and enjoys flying.

Smile

This poem tells a lot about what is important to its author. All of us become a little discouraged once in a while. One of the secrets of getting up when we're down is to begin smiling. We act like we feel, but we also feel like we act. And smiling does something for those around us, too. As Mimas puts it, "when someone is happy, you, too, are happy; and when someone smiles, you smile back."

Betsy Craig

"I am a native Iowan who fled the snow and cold some sixty years ago and have been a Californian ever since. Now retired both as an English teacher and a lawyer I live with my husband, an Air Force retiree, in the foothills north of Auburn, California. On our four acres, we keep ducks, half a dozen chickens and a pair of peacocks. Our days are also livened by a houseful of pets—three small dogs, eight cats, a pair of parakeets, and a canary-winged BeeBee parrot. All the animals provide poetry material.

"Volunteer work fills much of my time and I am also active as a lector at St. Luke's Episcopal church. Since I firmly believe that each year one should learn something new, I celebrated my 81st birthday [in 1984] by taking guitar lessons. Our human family consists of an adopted son and two daughters, all Colombians from the same family. While living with my husband in Japan I became interested in haiku [hay-COO] and it remains one of my favorite verse forms."

The Cat With the Cauliflower Ear

If you are quite young, you will probably find some words you don't know in this poem. I suggest you look them up and see how each one adds meaning. The poem has a purpose. Which line tells what it is?

Heads bobbing like corks

This is a type of poetry called haiku. The haiku poem is a word picture that does not require the subject and verb structure we expect for sentences. Haiku is fun because it has no repeated stresses. In fact it has seventeen syllables, and this number can't be divided by any other whole number greater than one.

Martha H. Daniel

Martha Daniel obviously cares about people. Before she retired she had been an administrative aide in the Catholic Charities program for the aged, and for three years she was employed as secretary for the Modesto, California office of the American Heart Association. Now she lives in New Mexico. She has been writing poetry for more than fifty years.

Julie Dansby

Julie was fourteen (in 1985) when she sent me her contributions for this collection. She was a high school freshman in Prattville, Alabama and played on the girl's basketball team. She began writing poetry when she was seven or eight and likes to send her poems in greeting cards for family and friends. She collects old records and teddy bears.

Delores Davis

To provide a "beautiful and educational mental excursion for appreciative readers" is why Delores Davis writes. She lives in Tucson and teaches preschoolers.

Body Parts

This poem is obviously not just to read. A parent or teacher recites the poem while doing the motions with the children. After going through it a few times, children will learn the words and the actions.

Marianne Filby

Marianne Filby is managing editor of the *Antioch Review* which is associated with Antioch College in Yellow Springs, Ohio. In one of her letters, she explains why she writes poetry.

"I have always made up simple poems to amuse my children and finally began writing them down when my youngest became enamored with word games. Reading should be fun at the early level and most young children are fascinated by rhythm and rhyme, especially if it incorporates ideas they can laugh at or relate to personally. I also use it as an escape from all the "serious" writing I am subjected to at the *Review*. I guess I am a middle-aged lady with the soul of a small boy."

Pet Names

Have you ever thought of giving your pet an unusual name—
something different from the common Brownie or Spot? My family once
had a cat we called Molly (short for molecule because she was small).
Bloopers seemed to fit a beagle dog we once had. In this poem you can see
that Freckle-head thought it was O.K. to be different. Children
sometimes object to having unusual names, but pets never seem to mind.
By the way, the straw used to make brooms before most of them were
made with plastic bristles is called broomcorn.

Lillian M. Fisher

After twelve years teaching public school, Lillian Fisher spent five
more years teaching art in her own studio. Now she directs a writer's
group in the Southern California town of Alpine where she lives with
her professor husband. Her poetry and prose are frequently published.

Barefoot I Go

This poem touches a human experience people like to remember.
Lillian Fisher told me in her letter, "I have never forgotten what it was
like to be a child. I loved summers when I could run about without
shoes."

To read it aloud, I would begin at a normal pace; then pick up a little
excitement at line four to emphasize the running.

Little Chick

What makes you like this poem? I especially like two things. First the
poet is talking *to* the little chick, not about it. Can you imagine yourself
holding a baby chick and telling it things it can't understand? Second, I
like the poem's repetition of "smooth and brown." Usually, repeated
words make bad writing because they distract the reader. But here they
are used to deepen an impression.

Sea Horse

You can learn interesting habits of the sea horse just by reading this poem. If you want to write a poem and aren't sure what it will be about, why not look in an encyclopedia or a science book to learn about some interesting creature like the baboon or the bald eagle. Make a list of characteristics. Then see how many of them you can weave into verse. Try to have a main thought to give your poem unity. Can you identify the idea that keeps "Sea Horse" from falling into unrelated pieces?

Ann Gasser

"Until 1981 I spent most of my spare time sewing, doing many kinds of art work—practically anything creative. I wrote and directed plays for church programs and for eight summers created phono-sync productions for children who appeared in the Children's Theater on Steel Pier in Atlantic City, New Jersey. Following an injury incurred while painting scenery for a local community project, I developed back problems. I discovered to my delight that poetry and verse make a terrific creative outlet when back pain makes activity difficult. My husband is most supportive of my new interest."

Ann Gasser is now co-host with Mary Ann Bandemer for a local cable television program called "Poets' Pause." The two have published a book of limericks. Other books are in the works.

Janet Geiger

As an only child of highly intelligent, accomplished parents, Janet Geiger developed a deep respect for the giants of classical music and of literature whom she felt inadequate to follow. Her poetry came through a desire to help her own children feel "at home" in the world. One of her poems which we published in *With Joy*, an earlier book, is entitled "Mean."

We shiver when we think of
People, when they're old,
Who have no one to love them
Or protect them from the cold.

And tears come if we listen
To someone, as they tell,
Of a puppy that is frightened
And not treated very well.

Of all the things we hear of
And each thing we have seen
The hardest act to understand
Is something very mean.

We cannot see this "Meanness."
It lives behind the face.
Like the wick inside a candle,
It's in a hidden place.

How do we live with meanness?
It's painful, to be sure,
It really is a sickness,
Do you know the cure?

Clouds

When Janet Geiger's son, Steve, was seven, his friend next door died of leukemia. Many evenings she sat outside in a rocking chair with Steve helping him overcome fears of darkness, death and sickness. She wrote "Clouds" to help him understand. Steve is now a dentist in Atlanta.

With that background, can you see more meaning in the poem? Writing a poem is one way to tell someone something very important.

Howard Goldsmith

I was delighted to receive Howard Goldsmith's contribution to the collection because he provided two excellent poems for my first collection. Here is one of them. Its title is "The Wind."

> I am the wind,
> Raging through the roaring billows,
> Purring through the pussy willows.

> I am the wind,
> Scaling the highest mountains,
> Splashing water in the fountains.

> I, the wind,
> Toss and bellow
> As I strew the leaves, all gold and yellow.

> From my breath,
> The clouds all scurry,
> Papers scatter in a flurry.

> When I sigh,
> The raindrops dance,
> Honeybees on flowers prance.

> When I rest,
> The earth grows still,
> As I nestle on a hill.

Howard has authored some forty books for children including *Toto the Timid Turtle* and *The Twiddle Twins' Haunted House*. He lives in Flushing, New York and enjoys classical music and old films.

Old Steam Train

Many years ago, trains were different from the way they are now. Locomotives ran on steam. Most of the sounds they made were not like today's train noises. In Howard Goldsmith's poem, you can hear the old steam engine "chugging down the track." Find where the rhyming words are in each verse.

Dorothy Golub

Dorothy Golub has been an elementary school teacher and loves children. She would like to see them enjoy poetry as much as she always did.

Hop-toad

" 'Hop-toad' came about when I saw a toad hopping and jumping in a park. A boy who also saw him, started to hop. This brought to my attention the fact that while a boy can hop and jump like a toad, a toad cannot run and skip like a boy."

Bedtime

"This poem expressed my own personal feelings. When I was a youngster, I never liked to go to bed. I felt it was a waste of time which could be better used for an adventure or for having fun. I put it in the mouth of a boy, and there you have it."

La Donna Lane Grigsby

La Donna was seven when she wrote her first poem for a second-grade class assignment. Here is "The Chase":

> Said the cat to the bee,
> "I'll win the race, as you'll see."
> The bee won, and the cat was stung;
> That was the end of the chase.

Off and on since, she has put words into verse. Not long ago, her thirteen-year-old daughter encouraged her to pick up writing again.

She works as a convenience store clerk. At home she gardens and raises rabbits.

Bug watching

This bug poem reminds me of another nice one by Carol Schema. It's called "Little Spider." You would almost get the idea that the two authors were watching the same bug.

> Just a wee brown speck
> On the web
> That's hanging there,
>
> Slowly dropping now,
> Seemingly
> Floating on air.
>
> Then on spindly legs
> It lands lightly
> On the wood floor,
>
> And suddenly with speed,
> Scurries off
> To be seen no more.

Nikki Grimes

Nikki Grimes has an interesting and varied history. She grew up in New York City. She taught creative writing and socio-linguistics at Rutgers University in New Jersey. She has lived in Dar es Salaam, Tanzania while studying Swahili literature, and in Stockholm where she lectured on Black English and Black literature.

Her artistic talent has been expressed in radio journalism, photography and radio production as well as in poetry and other kinds of writing. Two of her books, *Growin'* and *Something on My Mind*, have received top ratings by reviewers.

Another book report is due

I always enjoy hearing sincere people of other cultural groups talk. This prayer is written so realistically that it almost comes alive. It also clearly shows the closeness of a spiritual relationship.

127

The poem is from a collection entitled, "Dear God, Remember Me." Nikki Grimes said it was all right to let you see another of the prayers in this collection:

We need space, God,
just a little.
We're so many,
seems there isn't any room to grow.
I don't know.
Don't mind being close sometimes,
but three in a bed gets kinda tight,
and I always end up having to fight
for cover.

My mother says that one day we'll move
to a bigger place.
But, right now it would help
if we had just a little more space.
And Lord,
how about an extra bed?

Babs B. Hajdusiewicz

"I enjoyed seven years of classroom teaching prior to three years as Director of Special Education in school districts in Indiana and Michigan. I then combined motherhood with teaching at the university level. In 1979 I founded Pee Wee Poetry, a language experience program for two-to-six-year-old children.

"My interest in poetry for young children began years ago. While working with mentally impaired children who functioned in the preschool range, I found that poetry was an extremely effective medium for teaching any subject matter. This led me to believe that preschool children would enjoy poetry. Pee Wee Poetry is growing annually with added staff.

"I began to write poetry when I found an absence of quality poems to 'speak to' specific areas of interest to children. Since one of those areas, seat belt and car seat usage, had not yet been explored in poetry, I wrote a collection of poems designed to instill the values of car safety in young children.

"In addition to editing two community organization newsletters, I avidly enjoy collecting and restoring antiques. I like to do many forms of creative needlework, sewing and woodworking. My husband and I, with our elementary-school age children, Nick and Alison, enjoy traveling."

Blankie's Shampoo

Written after the poet watched her young daughter lament the washing of a much-loved blanket.

My Turn to Talk

Preschoolers aren't the only ones who can identify with the bit of life drama in this verse.

My Organs

"Most states have mandated that children aged four and under be belted into a special seat in vehicles. The poem, 'My Organs,' was written to encourage the newly-turned five-year-old to continue to practice good car safety rules."

The Rudes

This poem could help children understand a character-development concept not always obvious to them without adult counsel and example.

Using unkind words is one way people can be rude. Here is a poem Mrs. Hajdusiewicz wrote about words that hurt:

> We can shut up a box,
> A window or door,
> But when speaking to humans,
> We need to think more.
> A box is just paper.
> A door has no ears.
> A window is glass.
> Not one can cry tears!
> But a human's a person
> With feelings and such,
> And a "shut up" hurts feelings
> So-o-o-o very much!

Robert D. Hoeft

Robert Hoeft teaches English at the Blue Mountain Community College in Pendleton, Oregon. In addition to teaching the usual classes in composition, literature and such, he helps students know how to write poetry, fiction and drama. Here is how he describes his life:

"I'm married with a going-to-college daughter and son. I don't hunt or fish or go bowling on Wednesday or paint or sculpt or collect string or carve soap. I teach until school is out, and then I try to write in the summer. Over the years I've cranked out novels, short stories, plays and lots and lots of poems. I really have a rather dull life. My good lines and ideas end up in poems, and my friends must think I'm bland. Perhaps they are right, but that is a brighter prospect than being witty in person and boring in print."

One of Mr. Hoeft's poems, "If Things Grew Down," was read on a BBC television program and appears in a 1986 Scott Foresman textbook.

One-eyed Teddy

What do you suppose ever happened to the teddy bear that lost an eye? Well, Wallis Adams wrote a poem about just such a bear. Of course, she didn't know anything about Mr. Hoeft's poem, but you can imagine that the two poems are part of the same story. Here is "Old Teddy."

My teddy bear is old and torn
And only has one eye,
But if I couldn't find him
When I go to bed, I'd cry.

He is the best friend I have
In every single way,
And with his stuffing in or out,
We are friends to stay.

Would you like to see another Robert Hoeft poem? This one is called "Losing Things."

I can lose just about anything
Even a sandwich of jelly or jam.
My toys turn invisible
Every chance they can.
My shoes hide in my closet;
My socks hide under my bed.
Mamma says I'd lose my ears
If they weren't attached to my head.
I've lost my favorite wagon;
I've lost my favorite book.
But I'll never, NEVER, lose me
'Cause I always know where to look.

Andrea Keremes

"I have always enjoyed writing poems. As a child, I was forever playing with words, rhymes, and rhythms. My love for poetry has grown over the years. Today, as an editor of elementary school textbooks, I often have the opportunity to write both poems and stories for children. I always write with children in mind. I want to share with them all the beauty, delight, and mystery I see in the world around me."

Babysitting

"I wrote 'Babysitting' after watching a young boy helping care for his new baby sister. He was at first a bit unhappy and bored with his responsibility, but gradually warmed up to his new little friend. The poem should be read with a somewhat droning, bored voice for the beginning lines. The ending should, of course, be read with quickened pace and liveliness."

Raindrops

"Raindrops was written one chilly, rainy night in autumn. It was miserable outside, but I was snug and warm in my house. It was so glorious to hear the happy tap-tap-tapping of the drops of rain on my roof and window that I just had to write a poem about the happy sound!"

Robert King

Grand Forks, North Dakota, where Robert King lives, is on the Red River of the North. He helps students at the University of North Dakota learn how to write better. He also teaches elementary school teachers how to teach writing. Besides being a university professor, he sometimes travels around the state spending a week at a time in various schools helping children learn to write poetry. He has three children of his own and likes to hike, camp and swim with his family.

Lion

Mr. King says that "Lion" is an imaginary poem because he has never been chased by a lion. He imagined someone seeing something they weren't sure was a lion. He wrote down the first line: "I think that's a lion." Then he thought about what could follow as he figured out what the rest of the poem could say.

In reality, lions in the wild seldom attack people, but facing a lion out in the open would frighten almost anyone.

I like this poem because it shows what can happen when we worry. As we think what might be and what might happen, our mind can play tricks on us. We can begin to believe that what we fear is actually about to occur. Of course we really should be careful and sometimes even fearful, but it's sad to see someone afraid without a good reason. If you are easily frightened, maybe you can understand a little better by reading about the child in the poem that began to see a lion in the grass.

What do you think makes people unnaturally afraid? How can you help someone who has too many fears?

As you read this poem aloud, let your voice show more and more excitement climaxing with the last two words. Not all poems rhyme. Does this one?

For fun, you might like to try writing an acrostic. Robert King explains how: "Write the name of an animal *down* one side of the page. Those letters start each line of your poem. Think of words that start with the letters of the word you chose and write your poem." For example:

> L ying in the grass is a lion.
> I see him.
> O h! He sees me!
> N ow I'd better leave!

You could try the word "bear" or any other one you like. It's best not to write in this book.

B ———————————————

E ———————————————

A ———————————————

R ———————————————

Giraffe

Robert King really did see a baby giraffe hiding under its tall mother giraffe and peeking out to see if people had gone away.

Do you like poems with short lines like this one?

Bonnie Kinne

"Much of my life has been involved in some way with children. My husband and I are the parents of five, now grown, and the grandparents of three. I've taught Sunday School for many years and also enjoyed working with Cub Scouts as den mother. After my children were in school I returned to college for a degree in education and taught for eight years.

"I've always tried to influence children to read for enjoyment and to write stories and poetry. I guess I got the message across because one former student admitted to my son that I had gotten her 'hooked on books.' Another youngster introduced me to her parents thus, 'Meet Mrs. Kinne. She's a poetry nut!' "

Bonnie Kinne's stories and poems have been published in several magazines. One of the reasons I like her bath poem is because it's short. I also like her poem entitled, "Hiccups." Maybe you will, too.

> You can't stop at one
> For once they've begun
> On and on they come.

Chasing Bubbles

When we talk we say some words or parts of words a little louder than others. Here is a sentence from "Chasing Bubbles" with the louder parts in darker print: "**I'm** a **speed**boat, **I'm** a **sub**." Try saying these words making the parts in lighter print louder. It doesn't sound right does it? Also, notice that only part of the word "speedboat" is louder.

Every word is made up of one or more sounds. The sounds are called syllables. "Speedboat" has two syllables. The first syllable is spoken more loudly. We say it is accented.

Here is another sentence not from our poem: "David is riding an elephant." The syllables "Da," "rid" and "el" should be accented. Repeat the sentence slowly to see if you agree. Now find the accented syllables in the rest of the poem. When words have two syllables, is the accent always on the first one? (Be careful.) How many accents are on each line in our poem?

Find some poems that do not have repeating patterns of accented sounds.

Vera Koppler

Most of the poems Vera Koppler has written are for adults. Many have been published. She wrote "Walking in the Rain" for her two oldest granddaughters. One of the things she especially enjoys is collecting picture postcards.

Joan Kramer

Joan Kramer is a professional writer living in McLean, Virginia (near Washington, D.C.). She writes mostly for newspapers. Her articles are usually about travel highlighted with her own photos, but recently she has also been writing poetry. Her husband is a consulting engineer. She enjoys a variety of activities, including baseball, cats, country music, crafts, fires, nautical antiques, trains, stained glass and the seashore.

To a Small Bear

If you didn't know the title to this poem, what clues would make you think it was about a stuffed toy bear? Why do you think Joan Kramer repeated the bear's name so often? What is the main point of what the child tells the bear? The problem is explained in the last stanza; how did the earlier stanzas prepare you to understand it? What concern not directly stated in the poem do you think might be solved for the child by a change in the bear's name?

By the way, a toy bear much like Theodore actually belonged to the Kramers' son, Andrew.

Lois Kromhoff

"My home is on a hill overlooking Lake Okanagan in British Columbia, Canada. I often see deer, bears and coyotes. In the winter, I put on cross-country skis at my garage door and enjoy afternoons in the woods. In the summer, I canoe and swim in the lake. My Shetland sheepdog enjoys the runs and the rides, but he would rather not swim."

Lois Kromhoff writes plays based on folklore and sometimes talks to groups of children or conducts poetry workshops for them at the local library. Most of all she likes to write poems. Some are published and some just shared with her young friends.

Stinker and the Bandits

"My 'Stinker' poem is based on reality. One Halloween, my son Jonathan and I were at our summer cottage by Cultus Lake. There were only three children near his age, and very few neighbours for 'trick or treat.' Boring? His three friends helped us dress the dog in a football shirt, then we bobbed for apples. While we were drawing pictures in the dark, we heard a scuffle at the door. It was Stinker and the bandits!"

Sharon Kuebler

"I still have a copy of my first poem, written in the first grade. Through the elementary grades and high school I continued to write—mostly poetry. Raising children brought my writing to a temporary standstill until recently when I decided to combine the two. Hence writing for children. Nothing short of a warm hug from two small arms gives me more pleasure."

Mrs. Kuebler also enjoys painting, sewing, gardening and tennis. She has four daughters.

Because I Am a Child

"This poem is about me, even though I am 38 years old. Among other things, I have been a horse, a bunny, a squirrel, and a boy ten years old. Like a child, I can pretend to be anything I want to be. The only difference is that I record my experience on paper in the form of a poem or story. So, in using imagination, I haven't grown up much since I wrote my first poem, and I hope I never do!"

For fun try using Sharon Kuebler's pattern, and write a verse telling what you might like to be. Lines below show you where to fill in your own words. But use a sheet of paper. It's best not to write in a book others might want to read.

If I were a _____
   I'd play all day

_____

I'd _____
   and _____
   and _____
But most of all I'd _____
   because
That's what _____ do best
If I were a _____

If you enjoyed this poem, you might also like Helen Bradford's "Just Me."

I think I'd like to be
                    a caterpillar
All fuzzy and wriggly
Scampering around in a tree,
    But a bird might eat me!

So I think I'd rather be
                    a bird.
I could fly up to the sky
Or hop across the lawn.
    But a cat might get me!

So I think I'd rather be
                    a dog.
Maybe I could find a boy to follow.
But then I couldn't ride a bike
    Or even climb a tree!

So I really want to be
                    just me!!

Martha Clark Lentz

Martha is a folk artist who lives with her husband and two boys in Wilmington, North Carolina. She loves the outdoors and enjoys camping with her family.

Quiet Friend

"Several very old and very large oak trees grew near where I live. One night I decided to paint them, and that evening I wrote the poem, 'Quiet Friend.' I had planned to make sketches the next day, but unfortunately my sons came down with the flu and I spent several days inside with them. When I finally left the house and drove down the

138

street where the oak trees had stood for hundreds of years, they were gone! The county had cut down every last one of them so they could widen the road. Now I have a poem but no painting. The most beautiful oak trees I've ever seen are gone forever.

"You may read my poem with sadness in your voice and a tear in your eye."

Thomas Lynn

"I write poems, songs, short stories, humorous articles, and essays—none of which are as yet destined for immortality. I am the father of six, grandfather of two, and husband of one. I am a recently retired federal agent and my writing interests take up nearly my entire time. (I treat it as a job.) I love to write children's poems and stories."

Cold Blows the Wind

Poetry is creative expression of ideas. The beauty and emotion of poetry depend on more than the technical meaning of the poem's words and phrases. Sounds, arrangement of the printed words, and the use of repetition help form the thoughts and feelings the poet wants to give the reader.

In reading this poem, let your voice emphasize the cold wind and the child's determination for protection. Stress your vowel sounds and change your speed of reading, as appropriate. To read a poem well to someone else, go over it several times yourself becoming familiar with the words.

Thomas Lynn gives some interesting background: " 'Cold Blows the Wind' is a very simple poem in quatrains [four-line stanzas] and reminds of our most recent winter here in Georgia. It wasn't of blizzard impact but sufficiently cold to warn of that possibility. Stanzas one, two, five and six include my observations of this past winter while stanzas three and four were borrowed from memory of the winters back in Missouri. We Georgians are not used to wind that blows icy cold and when we do experience it, we are likely to be quite impressed with Mother Nature."

Auril McKenzie

I discovered Auril McKenzie through her mother Auril Wood who has also contributed to this collection. They both live in the Sierra foothills about a hundred road miles north of my own home. Here is her response to my request for information:

"I am a watercolorist as well as a poet and live on a wooded property with abundant flora and fauna [plant and animal life]. Folk dancing, singing and playing the piano are some of the things I enjoy. I also like to read and travel.

"Recently I began working with handicapped adults teaching creative sewing, singing, poetry, crafts and stained glass. Mother and I have published a small collection of our poems titled *To Bridge the Gap*, which I also illustrated."

Conversation

This poem is in free verse. It has no rhyme or meter (repeated pattern of stronger sounds). Still you probably enjoyed it. Its nineteen words carry a lot of meaning.

Here are some questions to help you think it through. In the first stanza, what comes around the corner? Which of the following terms could describe the conversation you "hear" in the second stanza? lively, matter-of-fact, sad, interesting, respectful, cautious. At the third stanza—surprise—your mind probably replaced it's first picture with a different one. Do stanzas one and two still agree? The poem is about chickens, but what else is described by comparison? Did the chickens notice you sitting there near the corner of the house? What does this tell you about the conversation?

Angie Monnens

Well over four hundred of Angie Monnens' poems have appeared in print (and she's busy cranking out more). In her letter, she told me, "The years while my children were growing up were very happy and fulfilling. I raised such lovely children with the help of their kind father, who passed away just a year ago." Angie's home was full of life with six children, and obviously full of love and care, too. Moms and dads have much to do with how the kids turn out.

I Like to Dream

"I wrote this poem on a lovely day in May a number of years ago to become part of my opening article for the weekly columns I write for two local newspapers. In it I expressed fond memories of my childhood days, dreaming about the end of the school year coming up and the wonderful days of summer vacations.

"Back then no television sets kept us kids indoors, and so we spent every spare moment playing outside. I remember lying under a tree drinking in the wonders of nature.

"Our mother taught us to find God's love in the magic of His works. She firmly believed we could never be truly unhappy if we took advantage of the beauty that surrounds us. And she was right."

Mrs. Monnens has pointed out the value of pausing to observe and think. However, dreaming that becomes an escape from reality and responsibility can lead to a ruined life.

Eileen Ellen Murphy

"I'm semi-retired from a government job. I've written mostly for children. I like cats and dogs, but find cats easier to write about."

Fourteen Cats

What is the rhyming pattern in this poem? In which stanza is the pattern a little different? This poem is fun to read aloud.

Nora Norton

When Eleanor Louise Norton's children started growing up and leaving home, she went to college and found she enjoyed writing. She has worked for a local newspaper interviewing people for a weekly feature section and writing police and fire reports.

She loves to read, and she often helps decorate the bulletin board or teach a Sunday School class at the Baptist church she attends.

Mud

What words help you "hear" the action of this poem?

When Bonnie Kinne learned that her poem, "Chasing Bubbles," was to appear on the same page with one entitled "Mud," she shared one she wrote with the same title:

> Mud is just dust
> Taking a bath
> In a puddle
> Of rain water.

Nita Penfold

Bonita Penfold Raquet has been writing since the age of ten. Seventy of her poems and a short story had already appeared in a number of publications when she submitted "Bus Ride" for this book. She has studied communications, education and writing, and is co-editor for *Earth's Daughters*, a periodical published in Buffalo, New York.

Bus Ride

"The poem 'Bus Ride' came out of a ride with a group of preschoolers. They all wanted to sit in the back because of the 'bumps' and I remembered doing that as a child on the school bus. As I listened to the rhythm of the bus noises, the poem came."

Louis Phillips

Louis Phillips, born in 1942, is an active playwright currently teaching creative writing at the School of Visual Arts in New York City. He and his wife, Patricia Ranard, have twin sons, Ian and Matthew.

Advice

You may have heard the lines, "If at first you don't succeed, try, try again." This poem reminds me of that "advice." Why do you think Louis Phillips repeated "& another" so many times?

Debbie Rose

"I live and work in Providence, Rhode Island. I currently have two jobs I enjoy very much. One is at a record store and the other at the Trinity Square Repertory Company where I am a house assistant. When I'm not working, I usually spend my time writing and listening to music. I'm 23 years old [in 1986] and have been writing since I was 12. Writing for children refreshes my love and awe of simple things and the playfulness of a child's life."

Playing in Puddles

"Most children love to splash and wade in water. When I see children jumping into puddles after a summer shower I know how much fun they're having because I once enjoyed the very same thing."

What do you find interesting about the pattern of this poem?

Robert D. San Souci

Since his early college years, Robert San Souci has been contributing short stories, articles and reviews to various periodicals. He has written several children's books, including *The Legend of Scarface*, which his artist brother, Daniel, has illustrated. Until recently he has been on the marketing staff in the San Francisco office of a major publisher. He is now a full-time free-lance writer.

Erica . . . ME

This is one of a series of five poems spontaneously inspired by pencil sketches drawn by a friend. The portrait of a girl standing on tiptoes in front of a full-length mirror started a train of thought about growing up, and eventually resulted in the poem.

Here is a spark for some serious thinking. Everyone gets older and will look different in future years. Discussion could lead to the idea of character formation. People are more than the way they look; and the foundation of character is laid in childhood.

Richard L. Sartore

Teaching and counseling with individuals of varied ages and circumstances have inspired most of Richard Sartore's writing. The poems, "Cat Tricks" and "Scared Silly," reflect his experience with elementary school youngsters. He has been a school counselor and administrator and is now Grants Coordinator for the Cerebral Palsy Center for the Disabled.

I asked him if he might be disabled himself, and he explained that he has multiple sclerosis. He "writes" by talking because he has no use of his legs and very little use of his arms and hands. Helpers copy his words. Mr. Sartore's home is in Clifton Park, New York.

Marion Schoeberlein

Marion Schoeberlein's home is in Elmhurst, Illinois. She works as a secretary and has particularly enjoyed writing for children's magazines.

Mrs. March

This poem was written for a friend's son. Both he and Marion Schoeberlein are lovers of nature.

Pearl Bloch Segall

Writing poetry began as an experiment for Pearl Segall when she was conducting a story hour for first and second graders. She would make up poems as "seeds" to get the children to express their feelings in verse. In the three years before submitting work for this collection, more than 200 of her poems had been published in some 60 periodicals and books.

Now that her four children no longer need her close attention she has returned to college at Kent State University for a degree in English education. She is editor of the school's literary magazine, *ICON*.

Wishful Thinking

A personal flashback to the author's own childhood days growing up in Chicago. I like the poem because it highlights the importance of being a friend to someone who needs companionship, rather than seeking only people who attract us.

Helen C. Smith

After teaching school for two years, Helen Smith went back to school herself and earned a Ph.D. degree. For over fifty years she served as a para-legal secretary in one law office in Evansville, Wisconsin. She enjoys sketching and painting as well as writing.

Etched in Black

"This poem came into being when I watched six hen pheasants walking alone through my garden. It always saddens me to hear the guns barking during the hunting season, for the male pheasants are beautiful birds."

Silly Sleep Sheep

Maybe you have heard that thinking of sheep jumping a fence and counting them will help a person go to sleep. Here is how Helen Smith explains her experience:

"I wrote about the 'silly sheep' in the early hours one morning following a sleepless night. Counting the sheep was my last resort, but even that did not work. Finally, in exasperation, I told the imagined sheep to go away. They were worthless to me. In trying to write my ideas on the matter, I thought of the sheep as just waiting to see whether I did what they do as they lay down. I have, on many occasions, watched sheep fold their forelegs in settling down to rest."

Rita Smith

Here is the "letter" I got with the first ten poems Rita Smith sent:

Editor:
>Hope you can find the time
>To read these words that rhyme.
>I have enough to fill a book.
>If you would like a closer look,
>Just let me know what you need,
>And I'll respond at top speed.

And my response (in part):

Rita:
>Yes, I found the time
>to read your lines
>>and make a few rejections.
>I made some marks
>upon your art
>>to show you my objections.

Rita Smith tells about herself: "I was born in Scotland and came with my husband to Colorado via Bermuda in 1969. One of the happiest days of our lives was when we became United States citizens. We are very proud and grateful Americans, and fly our flag every day.

"When my two daughters were small I always made up little rhymes to help them learn to dress themselves, count, spell, etc. Most of my poems are about the different stages of their lives. Now [in 1986], at 14 and 15, I think they appreciate having the trials and tribulations of these uncertain years expressed with a little humor."

Boring Baby

Rita Smith's pen is also handy for drawing pictures. Here is the one I found at the bottom of the manuscript page with her poem, "Boring Baby."

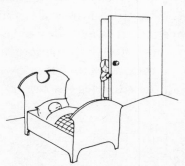

Glenda Stroup Smithers

—has taught second grade in Hickman Mills, Missouri for 15 years.
—conducts writing workshops.
—has been published in some 50 magazines.
—lives in the country with her husband, Steve, daughter, Kamber Jean, 3 horses, 3 dogs and 4 cats.

What's Inside?

"Those wrapped boxes are so mysterious. I don't mind birthdays like some older people do . . . because the presents are so much fun! People are like wrapped boxes, too. I am especially curious about children. They have a lot of mystery in them—hidden talents and dreams!"

Leaf Bed

"When I was a child I made leaf beds with my younger sisters, Sandra and Denise. I was the oldest so I pretended to be the Mom and would cover my sisters with a blanket of leaves. Most grown-ups don't lie in leaf beds—because of the bugs!"

Just for fun, would you like to see another poem about leaves? Nora Norton, whose poem, "Mud," appears in this book, also wrote "Leaves."

Leaves of orange, gold and red
Falling down into a bed—
A bed that soon will blow away,
When the wind comes out to play.
Leaves will tumble, leaves will fly
With no time to say good-bye.

Geoffrey Stamm

Geoffrey is a Vietnam veteran living in Mantua, Ohio.

The Color of Skin

"You might say my poem was inspired by the Hiram College Sociology Department and by the Christian Church (Disciples of Christ). Both organizations instilled in me a sense of social justice and taught me about human equality and dignity."

Dr. Donald Stoltz

Dr. Stoltz has been a physician in the Philadelphia area for over twenty years and has a large general practice. Because of his interest in children, he has written and illustrated several successful children's books and numerous short stories.

He is founder and president of the Norman Rockwell Museum in the Curtis Building in Philadelphia and is considered an authority on Rockwell's life and works. He is author of a popular three-volume set of Rockwell art books and a more-recently-published large book, *The Advertising World of Norman Rockwell.*

Ginger Ale

"Obviously, Norman Rockwell loved dogs as much as most people do who have them as pets. His incorporation of dogs in hundreds of pictures throughout his career certainly played a big part in the warmth that people feel when looking at his paintings and sketches.

"As for my personal experience with a dog, I do have a sheepdog named Friday which I have never been able to train to fetch the paper. Of course, this is probably better than having her bring back eight or nine as mentioned in the story."

Deborah Vitello

Deborah Vitello enjoys latch hook and ceramics. She plays the piano and the guitar. She draws and paints pictures. And she is a baker's assistant in a doughnut shop.

Bubbles Popping

As Deborah watched her daughters playing with soap bubbles, her thoughts went back to how she felt about bubbles in her own childhood, and she put her ideas into verse.

Balloon Moon

In concrete poetry, thoughts are expressed not only by the choice of words, but also by the unusual way they appear on the page. For fun, you might find another poem in this book (such as "Contented Fish" by Auril Wood or "Bath Time" by Bonnie Kinne) and copy the words as concrete poetry. You could even add art work.

Ted Wade

I must have been a preschooler when my mother introduced me to poetry. She had me learn Rose Fyleman's poem, "Mice." Maybe you'll like it, too.

> I think mice
> Are rather nice.
>
> Their tails are long,
> Their faces small,
> They haven't any
> Chins at all.
> Their ears are pink,
> Their teeth are white,
> They run about
> The house at night.
> They nibble things
> They shouldn't touch
> And no one seems
> To like them much.
>
> But I think mice
> Are nice.

Much has happened since then. I grew up, studied physics and earned a doctorate in education. I have worked as a teacher and administrator, and now, among other things, write about home schooling. My youngest (of three) was born over twenty years ago while my wife, Karen, and I were missionaries for the Seventh-day Adventist Church in Rwanda, Africa.

Life for me is inspired by the shepherd described in an ancient poem. Here are the first four lines. I think you know the rest.

The Lord is my shepherd;
I shall not want.
He maketh me to lie down in green pastures:
He leadeth me beside the still waters.

. . .

One Little Drum

After I began choosing material for this book, I decided it would be fun to string some of my own words into verse. As you read "One Little Drum," I hope you can hear the tat-a-tat and the marching feet. Read it out loud emphasizing the rhythm. Try tapping out the beat as you say the words.

Where, in the poem, do you first realize that the young drummer may be heading for trouble? What makes you think that his mom and dad might not have enjoyed the drum as much as he did? What is different about the last line, and what does this add to the meaning of the poem?

It's easy to think only of ourselves, forgetting to care about other people's happiness.

A string down the middle

I had originally intended to include in this book a section of riddle verses, and several people wrote some good ones for me. We changed that plan, but I have included just one of my own verses about something with a string down the middle. (No, I'm not telling you what it is.)

Would you like to see a guessing poem Angie Monnens wrote?

Choose a word
that just might fit.
If it doesn't,
think a bit.

Little squares
black and white.
Try again;
You'll get it right!

Emina Wesner

Mrs. Wesner began writing verses at age eight. Now she writes essays and children's stories as well as poetry. In addition to being an author, she is a musician and former teacher of piano. Her writing has been published in a number of magazines and books.

Woodpecker Hill

"When our home was first built, in a wooded suburban development, we were on Woodpecker Hill, literally. The ancient oaks and walnut trees held a bonanza for the 'red-headed residents,' and *we* were outnumbered. Sadly, as more houses came, more magnificent trees went down, and too many of the natives moved away. Still, memories are strong of the days when there was a 'wonderful racket on Woodpecker Hill'!"

Bicycle Parade

" 'Bicycle Parade' was written for and about First Grandchild Jennifer Joan—a lively redhead—in response to a 'What can I do?' plea. Actually, I was recalling a favorite Fourth-of-July celebration of my own childhood. Intended to picture a typical small-town (Independence, Missouri) Fourth of years gone by, I am amazed to realize that it is suddenly all relevant again—parades, picnics, fireworks and hot-air balloons! 'What it was like' quite unexpectedly has become 'what it is.' How refreshing!"

Martha E. Whittemore

"I am the wife of a retired minister. My life has been busy working with people in church activities. I love children, and story-telling has been my forte. I play the cello and have been active in music for many years. Now that I am less involved in these endeavors, I have time for writing. My poems and stories are based on life experiences of children."

Arabella

"The poem about Arabella was my own experience when I was three. Arabella was my favorite rag doll. I remember so clearly the morning my dad brought her in from being left outside, without her head. I was completely shattered and never cared about a doll much after that."

Mrs. Whittemore wrote another little poem I think you will enjoy. It's title is "Unhoed."

> I planted seeds,
> But up came weeds
> In my garden so new.
> I didn't hoe
> So had to mow,
> And never knew what grew.

Edel Wignell

Edel is a free-lance writer and compiler, aged 48 (in 1986), who lives with her husband in Melbourne, Australia. She writes articles, verse and stories for both child and adult markets. As can be seen in her poem, "The Catcher Caught," she enjoys playing with words and ideas.

The Catcher Caught

Often we use words in strange ways. For example, what do we "catch" about a cold? Can you think of some other things we say we catch when we really don't chase them? "Run" is another word with different meanings. Can you think of some things that run without feet? Can you "see" without using your eyes?

Auril Wood

"My ranch-style house in the Sierra foothills town of Magalia is surrounded by a forest of oak, pine, cedar, shrubs and, in season, wildflowers. Magalia was a roaring mining town during the Gold Rush days. The largest gold nugget found in California was discovered here.

"I am a retired school teacher with a special credential to teach disadvantaged children. The teaching years were a time of creative instruction and gave me much gratification.

"I have published articles, stories and poems in education, children's and church magazines. I also wrote a column about nostalgia and nature for a local newspaper.

"I quilt, knit, crochet and do embroidery; but my favorite activities are teaching an adult church school class and giving informal talks for church groups."

Terry Zabor

"I have used the name Terry Zabor for a number of years in business and in some unimportant circles. My legal name is Theresa Zaborowski. I am a young fifty years of age (in 1986) and have four children and one grandson. I enjoy my work as a bookkeeper.

"Most of my poetry is of a personal nature relating to things that are happening in my life. Because I like music and don't really appreciate prose, I often choose to write in meter and rhyme."

No More Kitten

Terry Zabor wrote this poem and "No One Came to Claim Him" about her own pets. Were you surprised to learn what happened to the kitten?

Index

INDEX